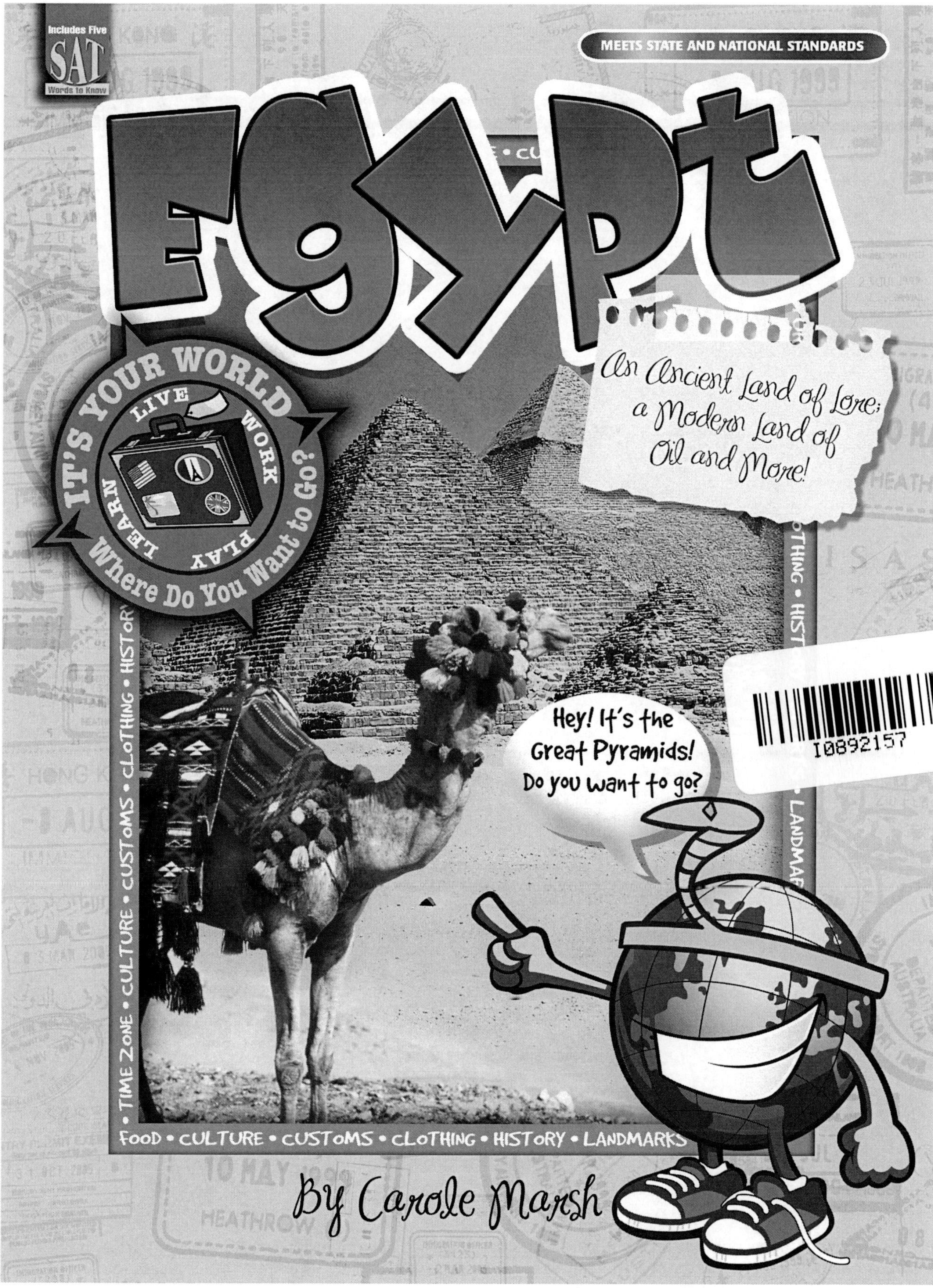
Includes Five SAT Words to Know
MEETS STATE AND NATIONAL STANDARDS
EGYPT
An Ancient Land of Lore; a Modern Land of Oil and More!
IT'S YOUR WORLD
LIVE
WORK
PLAY
LEARN
Where Do You Want to Go?
Hey! It's the Great Pyramids! Do you want to go?
TIME ZONE • CULTURE • CUSTOMS • CLOTHING • HISTORY
FOOD • CULTURE • CUSTOMS • CLOTHING • HISTORY • LANDMARKS
By Carole Marsh

Live • Work • Play • Learn

GALLOPADE INTERNATIONAL

Gallopade International is introducing SAT words that kids need to know in our books. The SAT words in this book have a gray box around them. Students can look up the definitions and increase their vocabulary. Happy Learning!

Gallopade is proud to be a member and supporter of these educational organizations and associations:

Association for the Study of African American Life and History
National Alliance of Black School Educators
American Booksellers Association
American Library Association
International Reading Association
National Association for Gifted Children
The National School Supply and Equipment Association
The National Council for the Social Studies
Museum Store Association
Association of Partners for Public Lands
Association of Booksellers for Children

At the time of publication, all websites referenced in this document were valid. However, due to the changing nature of the Internet, some addresses may change or the content become less relevant.

It's Your World Books

Africa: A Safari Through Its Amazing Nations!

Australia: The Land Down Under for Mates of All Ages!

Canada: The Maple Leaf Melting Pot Country!

China: A Great Wall Runs Thru It!

Egypt: An Ancient Land of Lore; a Modern Land of Oil and More!

France: The Ooh-La-La Country Everyone Loves!

Germany: The Country of Fairytale Castles and Cutting Edge Science!

Greece: A Volcanic Land of Ancient Olympic Origins!

India: Land of Six Senses and Intriguing Mystery!

Italy: The Country of Amazing Fountains and Awesome Arts!

Japan: An Island Country of Endless Intrigue!

Mexico: A Colorful Land of Exotic Culture!

Middle East: Ancient Countries of Current Events Headlines!

Russia: The Great Bear and Its Dramatic History!

South America: A Continent of Countries of Amazing Proportions!

United Kingdom: The Country of Ships, Sealing Wax, Cabbages, and Kings!

Other Carole Marsh Related Titles:

The Mystery of the Ancient Pyramid

Table of Contents

A Letter from the Author

From the desk of
CAROLE MARSH

Hey kids,

It's your world! It really, really is!
Of course, you already know that, don't you?
You surf the 'net, listen to satellite radio, watch television shows and movies set all around the globe—kids today are much more "worldly" than in the past, and that's a good thing!

Now's a great time to learn something about another country—such as Egypt. Why? Because one day, you might actually visit there (if you have not already!). You might go to school there—many colleges have ties with international schools around the globe. You might even go on to work in a foreign country!

Many companies have positions in other countries. Companies are "going global" as fast as they can. They have branch offices, manufacturing plants, and customer service centers scattered around the globe!

So, ready or not: YOU are a Citizen of the World! And you'll want to be a good one. How do you do that? You'll find out everything you can about that country, how it's the same, and how it's different from your own country. What language is spoken there? What customs do the people observe? What foods do they enjoy? What do they do for fun? What has happened in this part of the world and what is happening there now? It's fun ... and the more you learn the more you will enjoy whatever global opportunity comes your way!

This book is a good place to start your learning journey—so take advantage of the world—IT'S YOUR WORLD after all ... and guess what? It's a BIG world, after all!

Happy traveling and learning,

Carole Marsh
Always with passport in hand!

Why Should We Care About Egypt?

Egypt is home to one of the world's oldest civilizations as well as one of the world's oldest vacation spots! Early Greeks and Romans visited Egypt just for fun and to see the magnificent architectural wonders of early man! But Egypt is more than just pyramids and monuments. Egypt is a place of life, beauty, and excitement.

Since the end of the 19th century, Egypt has been evolving at a high speed. From hieroglyphs to computers, Egypt has been a leader in information technology in the Arab world. Today, Egypt is a mixture of modern skyscrapers, bustling cities, and ancient architecture!

One day, you might visit Egypt to see the Sphinx, cruise down the Nile River, live and work in Cairo, explore the pyramids, or take a journey through the Valley of the Kings. It could happen!

BREAKING NEWS!

In 2011, Egyptian citizens rose up against President Hosni Mubarak. Many Egyptians gathered to publicly demand democracy, a new government, and more power to the people. By June 2012, two of Egypt's most powerful forces were running against each other for the presidency: the military and the Muslim Brotherhood, an Islamist group. The Brotherhood stood for the people against President Mubarak. Thousands of Egyptians held their breath as they waited for the election results. On June 24, as thousands gathered in Tahrir Square, Mohamed Morsi, representing the Brotherhood, was named the winner and new president of Egypt.

Top Fast Egypt Facts!

Important facts to remember about the country of Egypt:

- Egypt is at the center of the Arab world.
- Egypt is officially called Arab Republic of Egypt.
- Egypt is Africa's second most populous country after Nigeria.
- About 95 percent of Egyptians live along the Nile River, on less than five percent of the land!
- Cairo is the capital of Egypt.
- The currency used is the Egyptian pound.
- The official language is Arab, although English and French are widely understood.
- The national anthem is "My Homeland."
- Egypt is the 16th most populous country in the world.
- Egyptians were among the first people to invent writing.
- The 365-day calendar and the 24-hour day are Egyptian inventions!
- The average age of Egypt's citizens is 24; this is very young; many young people want freedom to vote in open elections.
- June 24th, 2012, marks the day when the Egyptians officially elected their new president, Mohamed Morsi.

Ancient Egyptian Calendar

Now, you figure out the rest!

1. This is the Egyptian ___ ___ ___ ___.

2. The ___ ___ ___ ___ ___ ___ ___ ___ name of Egypt is the Arab Republic of Egypt.

3. Egypt is ___ ___ ___ ___ ___ ___'___ third most populous country.

4. The currency used in Egypt is the Egyptian ___ ___ ___ ___ ___.

5. The Egyptians created our 365-day ___ ___ ___ ___ ___ ___ ___ ___.

6. ___ ___ ___ ___ ___ is the capital of Egypt.

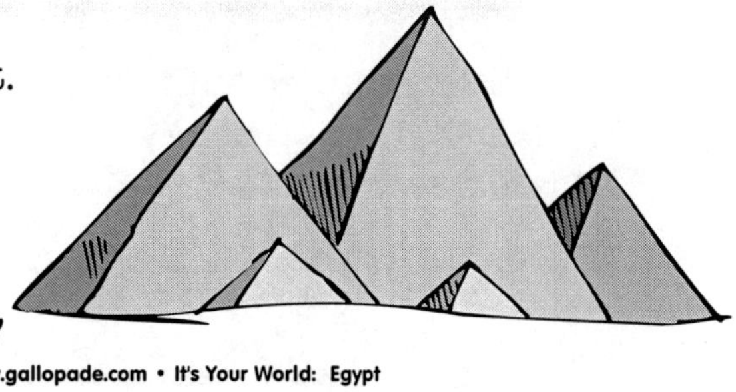

Where in the World is Egypt?

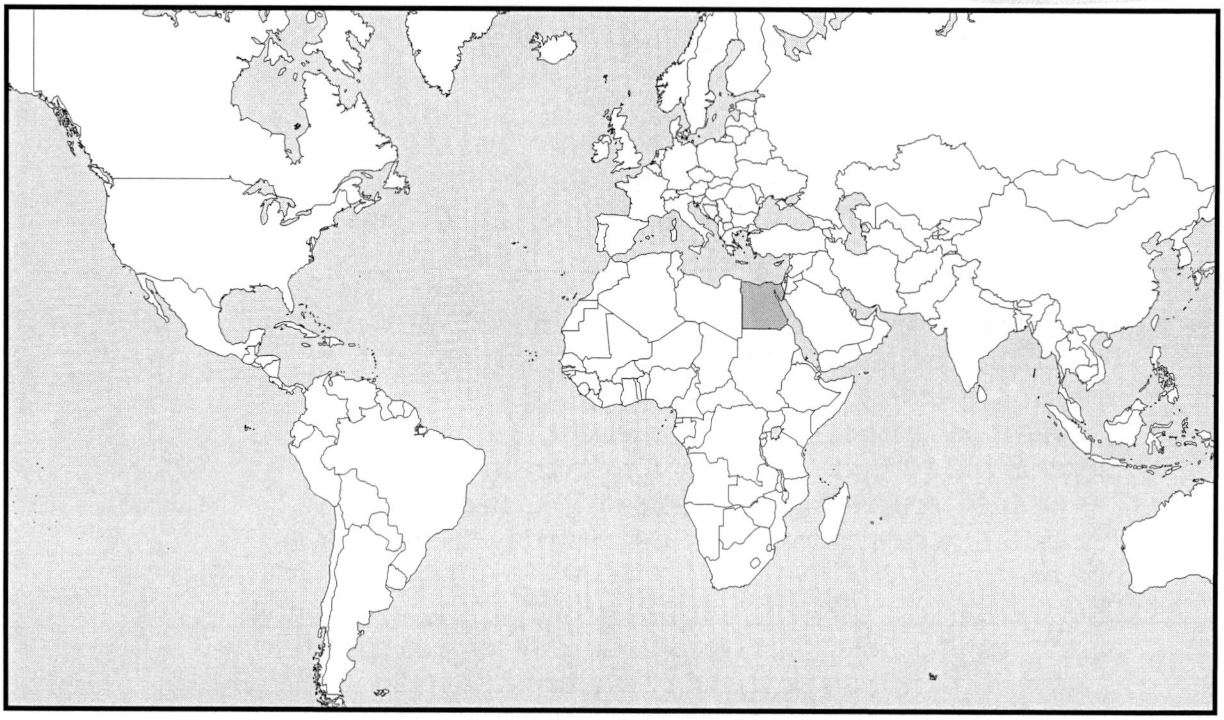

- Egypt is located in the northeast of the African continent.
- To the north, Egypt is bordered by the Mediterranean Sea and to the east by the Red Sea.
- There are four deserts in Egypt – the Libyan Desert, the Arabian Desert, the Nubian Desert, and the Sahara Desert.
- Egypt is divided into four main parts, which are the Nile Valley, the Arabian Desert, the Libyan Desert, and the Sinai.
- About 95% of Egypt is desert land!
- The Nile Delta is the only delta in Egypt and it is 100 miles long.
- There are five important oases in Egypt, all of which are located in the Libyan Desert.
- The climate in Egypt is hot and dry.
- There are only two seasons in Egypt. Winter lasts from December to March and summer lasts for the rest of the year!

Do You Know?

1. The Sahara Desert is almost the size of:
   a. Texas b. France c. The United States of America d. Rhode Island

2. The Nile River empties out into:
   a. The Mediterranean Sea c. Lake Nasser
   b. The Red Sea d. the Suez Canal

Ancient Egypt!

The ancient Egyptians believed that they were ruled by gods! They were actually ruled by kings called pharaohs (FAIR-ohs). The ancient Egyptians believed that the pharaohs were gods in human bodies. Sometimes the country was split into different regions and there were many different ruling kings at one time. Each family of kings was called a dynasty. Historians believe that there were at least 30 dynasties!

Egypt's ancient history is divided into three main periods. They are known as the Old Kingdom, the Middle Kingdom, and the New Kingdom. During the Old Kingdom, the great pyramids were built as burial chambers for the pharaohs. Great works of art and literature were created during the Middle Kingdom period. Egypt achieved its greatest power during the New Kingdom period. It had enormous power and conquered many other peoples.

Crosswords!

Use your new knowledge to fill in the crossword puzzle.

Across

3 Art and ________ were created during the Middle Kingdom period.

5 Ancient Egypt had at least 30 of these.

Down

1 A __________ was believed to be a god.

2 Pyramids were built during the ___ ______. (2 words)

4 Pharaohs ruled this country.

The Amazing History of Egypt!

Egypt is a beautiful country with a long and exciting history! In early Egypt, many different kings ruled the people. By the end of this period, writing had evolved and Egypt was unified into one kingdom. The Old Kingdom lasted for 500 years. During this time, workers built the first pyramids out of mud and bricks.

Alexander the Great

During the Middle Kingdom, pharaohs lost most of their power to rule local governments. When power was restored to the pharaohs, Egyptians returned to a time of wealth. In the Late Kingdom, Persia invaded Egypt.

Alexander the Great, a Greek warrior and king, was welcomed into Egypt after he defeated the Persian Empire. The Greeks ruled Egypt, and then the Romans took over! The Egyptians disliked the Romans and were not happy. During the Roman reign, Arabs conquered Egypt and Islam spread throughout Egypt.

Napoleon Bonaparte of France sailed to Egypt in 1790 and set up a ruling government in Cairo. In 1882, Britain gained control of Egypt. Egypt finally became an independent country early in the 20th century.

Today, Egypt is a modern country that thrives on its tourism industry. Egypt is an exciting place to visit and live!

Timeline!

Number these events in the order that they took place, first to last.

The year 2012 marked the first time Egyptians could vote freely for the president of their choice.

______Egypt was invaded by Persians.

______Napoleon Bonaparte sailed to Egypt.

______The first pyramids were built of mud and bricks.

______Egypt fell under the rule of the Greeks.

______Britian gained control of Egypt.

______Egypt was unified into one kingdom.

______Arabs conquered Egypt.

Famous Egyptian Folks!

Matching!

Match these famous Egyptian folks with their accomplishments

______1. When I came to power at the age of 18, I was highly educated and spoke many languages. I preserved Egypt's independence as a nation for over 20 years, despite the increasing power of Rome.

______2. I was given the throne at the age of eight or nine. As a pharaoh I accomplished little but I became one of the most famous pharaohs when my tomb was discovered. My tomb was the first found that was still intact and had not been robbed. Inside revealed an elaborate lifestyle that most people could only dream about.

______3. As playwright of the 1960s, I was associated with the golden era of drama in Egypt. I was also a poet. I was one of the greatest cultural figures of Egypt and the Arab world.

______4. I was the world's first named architect. I built Egypt's first pyramid which is still today one of the wonders of the ancient world. I was also a doctor, a priest, and a scribe.

______5. As the first pharaoh of the first dynasty in Egypt, I unified Upper and Lower Egypt into a single kingdom. I expanded the kingdom and developed trade links. My death at the age of 63 is a mystery. I was either attacked by wild dogs and a Nile crocodile or by a hippopotamus!

______6. I was a Greek man who established the last dynasty that would rule Egypt with the title of Pharaoh. The secret to my success was that I adopted the culture and became one of the people in Egypt. I brought Greek sciences and art to the Egyptian people.

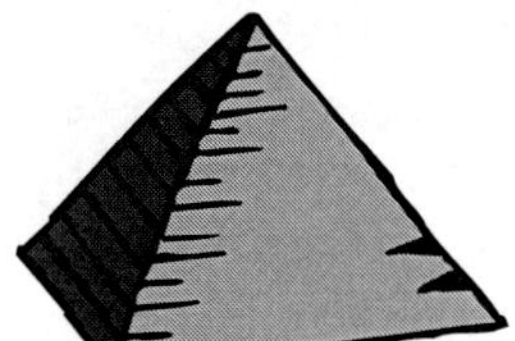

A. Imhotep

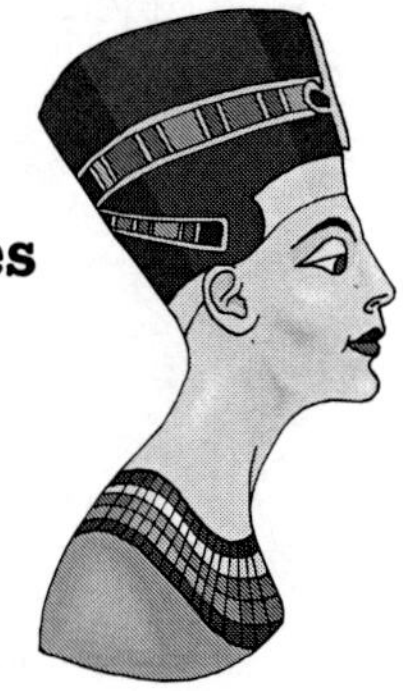

B. Menes

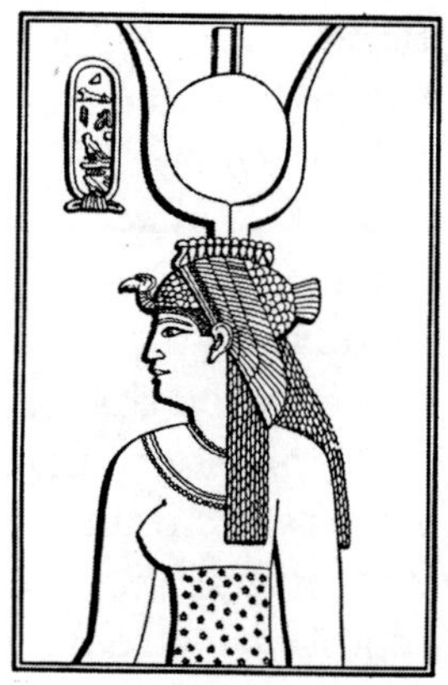

C. Cleopatra

D. Ptolemy

E. Alfred Farag

F. King Tut, or "The Boy King"

Guts and Glory Egyptian Style!

Mixed Up!
Match the paragraph to the word or phrase that the paragraph describes.

A. Embalming was practiced by the ancient Egyptians. All of the internal organs were taken out of the body except the heart. The brain was removed through the nose and thrown away! The body was dried out and then stuffed. The body was wrapped in linens with jewels and good luck charms between the layers.

______

B. Based on the image of a dung beetle, these were used by the ancient Egyptians to record historical events or to inscribe prayers to be placed on mummies to protect them from evil.

______

C. When Pharaoh refused to let the Israelites leave Egypt, ten bad things happened. Water turned into blood. Frogs, gnats, and flies covered the city. The livestock became sick. People developed boils all over their bodies. There were terrible thunder and hail storms. Locusts covered everything in sight and darkness fell upon Egypt for three days. The firstborn child in every family died.

______

D. In 1883, it was epidemic in Egypt. Diarrhea, vomiting, and leg cramps were the main symptoms. It spread among those living in unsanitary conditions. Rapid loss of fluids and dehydration caused many to go into shock and die.

______

E. Animal worship in ancient Egypt was part of daily life. This animal was sacred and respected. Egyptians first domesticated them 4,000 years ago! Soon, they were worshipped as gods. When this animal died, the family would go into deep mourning and would shave off their eyebrows as a symbol of grief.

______

CATS ______

CHOLERA EPIDEMICS ______

SCARABS ______

MUMMIFICATION ______

10 PLAGUES OF EGYPT ______

Egyptians Wrote in Hieroglyphs!

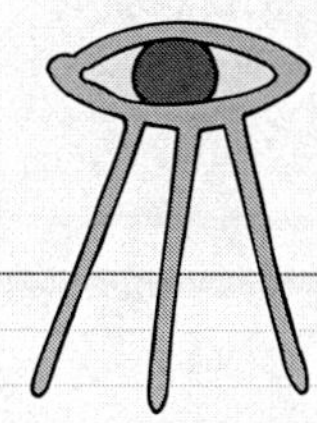

Did you know that ancient Egyptians developed the first form of writing almost 4,000 years ago? Egyptians used hieroglyphs, which means "the words of God." A hieroglyph was a simple drawing of a familiar object. Each hieroglyph represented a common object in ancient Egypt. They could represent the sound of an object or an idea associated with the object. Hieroglyphs were mainly used by priests.

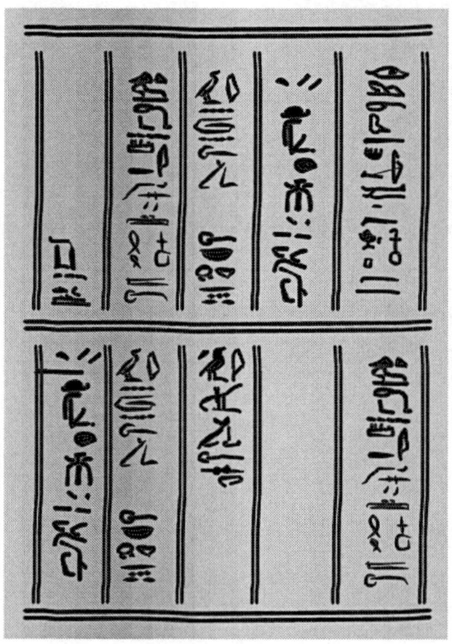

Over time, thousands of different symbols were used. This made it very hard for people to learn the language. One symbol alone could have up to three different meanings! Hieroglyphs were written in rows and columns and could be read from left to right or from right to left. The Egyptians knew which way to read the hieroglyphs by which direction the human or animal figures were facing.

Hieroglyphs were used for many different purposes. They were displayed on pyramids and tombs of royal families. Hieroglyphs were also used to tell the history of Egypt and the accomplishments and defeats of the pharaohs. They were also used on jewelry and nameplates.

Write Me!
Get out your crayons. Write a letter to one of your friends in hieroglyphs! See if your friend can figure out your message!

The Pyramids of Giza

The people of ancient Egypt believed that death was the start of a journey to the next world. Huge towers called pyramids were an important part of that journey. The body of a king was wrapped in special cloths and placed underneath or inside a pyramid to allow his journey to the afterlife.

In the Valley of Giza, three pyramids rise out of the dry desert sand! They were built by the order of King Khufu and his two sons, Kafhre and Menkaure. The Pyramid of Khufu is also known as the Great Pyramid of Giza. It covers a nine acre area and was built using more than 2 million limestone blocks. Each block weighed an average of 2.5 tons!

It took more than 20,000 workers over 20 years to construct the pyramids. King Khufu provided food and clothing for his workers. He was remembered as a great king for centuries for his kindness. Exactly how the pyramids were built is still a mystery. Many people believe that a ramp was built around a pyramid to wheel up materials. Others think workers lifted and pulled the rocks into place.

Word Play!

Because of its amazing construction, the Great Pyramid of Giza is known as one of the Seven Wonders of the Ancient World! See how many words you can create, big and small, with the letters in Great Pyramids of Giza.

GREAT PYRAMIDS OF GIZA

During the protests and demonstrations by the Egyptian people in early 2011, the famous pyramids historic site was closed to the public.

Tourism, a big economic factor in Egypt, was disrupted and many tourists fled the country and other people postponed trips to Egypt.

Many students from around the world attend school in Egypt.

Some historic digs were looted during the 2011 unrest; looters used this time to attack museums and steal gold and other artifacts.

It's a Lion—No, It's the Sphinx!

The Great Sphinx of Giza is a half-human, half-lion Sphinx statue that has represented Egypt for thousands of years. It is the largest monolith statue in the world. The Sphinx stands 241 feet long, 20 feet wide, and 65 feet high. It is located on the west bank of the Nile River. The Sphinx was carved out of the surrounding limestone bedrock. The Great Sphinx faces due east, with a small temple between its paws.

The time of construction is thought to be somewhere between 2520 BC and 2494 BC. It is thought by most Egyptologists to represent the likeness of King Khafra. It is believed that the Sphinx was originally painted and was quite colorful. Since then, the nose and beard have broken away.

The name 'sphinx' means 'strangler' and was first given by the Greeks.

Ancients knew the Great Sphinx as "Shesib Ankh" or "the living image."

Recently, the Sphinx has undergone a major restoration effort, done solely by Egyptians.

No other sphinx statue found in Egypt is either as old or as large as the Great Sphinx of Giza.

It is estimated the Great Sphinx weighs upwards of 200 tons.

Create your very own travel pamphlet.
Concentrate on an area that interests you. Perhaps you enjoyed learning about the people. Or maybe it was the monuments that interested you. Fold a piece of paper into three sections. This will give you six areas on which to put information.

Just Say No!

Customs and culture vary widely from country to country. Sometimes they vary in different regions of the same country. Here are custom and cultural differences observed by Egyptians!

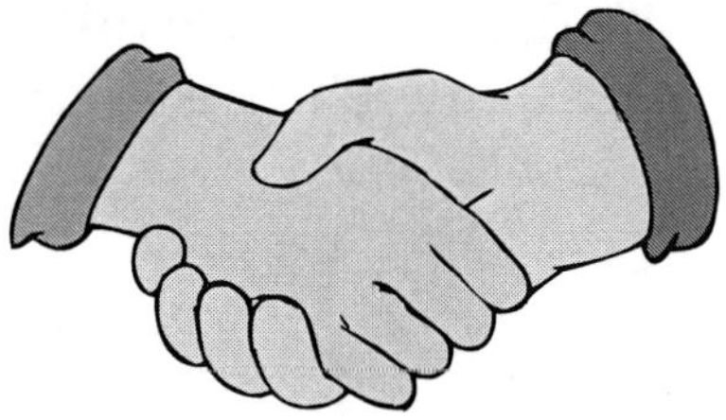

- The handshake is a common greeting. In a greeting between a man and a woman, the woman must extend her hand first.
- A gift must be offered with the right hand or, if it's heavy, both hands.
- Only your right hand can be used to eat.
- Women must dress modestly, with their legs and arms covered at all times. Some women wear a scarf that covers their face.
- The Ramadan holiday is celebrated by fasting (not eating) during the day, and feasting from sunset to early in the morning.
- Egyptian Muslims stop whatever they are doing to pray five times a day at exact times.
- Boys and girls are not allowed to socialize with each other or to date. Marriages are usually arranged by parents, or by an older woman called a "matchmaker."
- It is polite to refuse something the first time it is offered. If it is offered again, you can accept!

Create your own!

As we have seen, customs and cultural activities can help define who we are. Think about your family and friends and come up with some new customs for everyone to try.

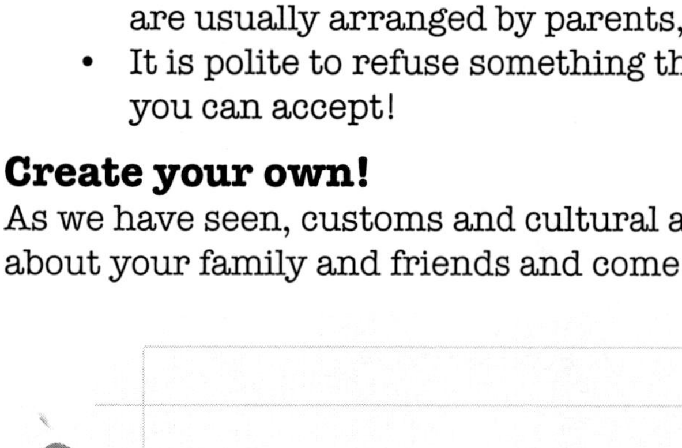

They Said No!

In early 2011, millions of Egyptians, especially young people and students, took to the streets to say "NO!" to a dictatorship type government and demanded new leaders elected in democratic elections. As the world watched, the people peacefully protested and refused to back down on their insistence for the rights of the people. Can you think of any other country that has revolted and just said "NO!" to an unfair situation that has gone on too long and has repressed the people?

Arabic? What's That?

The official language in Egypt is Arabic. They use a different alphabet. Their alphabet is the Arabic alphabet.

Match it up!
Below are some common Arabic phrases or words. See, if you can match them to the English word.

akhdar	March
ab	hot
harr	November
gadaa	salad
Adar	green
matihaf	red
la	lunch
Nofember	father
ahmar	museum
salata	no

Happy Holidays!

Egypt celebrates several holidays. Muslim Egyptians celebrate **Eid-al-Fitr**, the end of the holy month of Ramadan. During Ramadan, Muslims fast—do not eat food during daylight hours. Eid-al-Fitr is the most important holiday in Egypt and lasts for three days. People feast, exchange gifts, and pray.

Christian Egyptians have special religious holidays also. These include **Christmas** and **Easter**, but are celebrated on different days than in North America. For instance, Christmas Day is celebrated on January 7th rather than December 25th.

Other national holidays include **Revolution Day** (July 23rd), **Evacuation Day** (June 18th), **Armed Forces Day** (October 6th), and **Suez Day** (October 24th). On these dates, banks and schools are closed to commemorate these important days in Egypt's history.

Write it down!

Pretend you are visiting Egypt. Write a letter to your best friend. Tell him or her what it's like to celebrate Christmas in January. Did you get anything nice for Christmas?

Egypt on the Stage and in Museums!

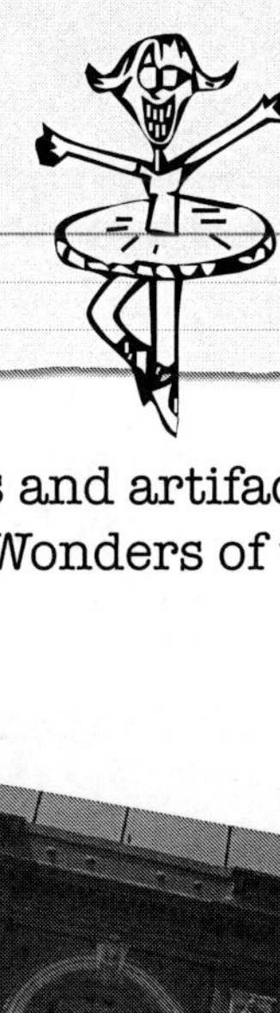

Most of what we know about ancient Egypt comes from paintings and artifacts in royal tombs. Egypt is home to the Pyramid of Khufu, one of the Seven Wonders of the Ancient world.

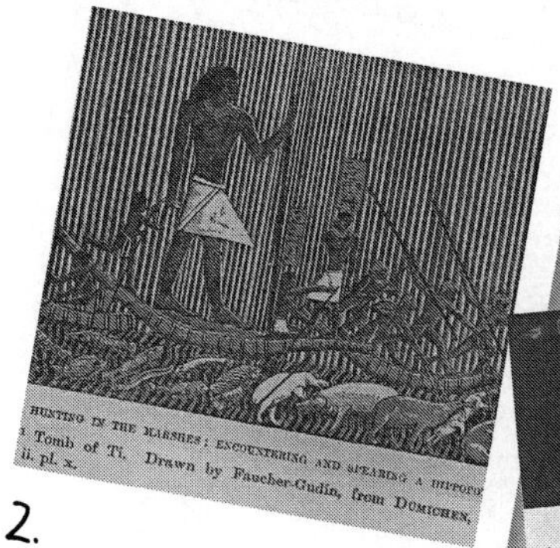

2.

3.

Notes

1. The Great Pyramid at Giza for King Khufu is the largest pyramid ever built.
2. This piece was painted in frontalist style. The head is drawn in profile, while the body is drawn from a front view.
3. The Egyptian Museum in Cairo exhibits more than 120,000 artifacts from the tombs of royalty.
4. The Egyptian version of Cinderella is considered the oldest account of the story.
5. This coffin was designed to hold King Tut's mummified internal organs.

1.

5.

4.

What's for Dinner?

Egyptians eat five light meals every day. Okra and aubergine are often used in their dishes. Desserts often include fruit. See what kinds of things there are to eat in Egypt. But be warned, Egyptians traditionally use their fingers to eat their meals!

Baba ghanouj is a dip made from aubergine (what we know as eggplant).

Couscous is a dish made of crushed grain that is steamed and served with lamb or chicken in a spicy sauce.

Molokhiyya is a summer vegetable often used to make a thick traditional soup.

Torly is a casserole or stew often made with lamb and mixed vegetables.

RECIPE

Always ask an adult for help when cooking!

Koshaf

INGREDIENTS

1 1/2 cups dried prunes
1 1/2 cups dried apricots
1 1/2 cups dried small figs (cut in halves)
2 1/4 cups raisins
1 1/2 cups sugar
3 3/4 cups water

MMMMMMMM...this was good!

DIRECTIONS

In a large mixing bowl, combine the dried prunes, dried apricots, dried figs, and raisins. Sprinkle sugar on top of the dried fruit mixture. Boil the water in a saucepan. Have an adult pour the boiling water over the fruit mixture. Stir the mixture well with a wooden spoon. Cover the mixing bowl, and place it in the refrigerator. Leave overnight for the best flavor. Serve in bowls as a dessert. Makes 6 servings.

Egyptian Football, Go Pharaohs!

There are still Pharaohs living in Egypt today! Instead of ruling the country, they play soccer, which is called "football" by the rest of the world! Football is a very popular sport in Egypt. The Egyptian Premier League is a professional league for the best players in Egypt. The Egypt National Football team is the Pharaohs. They wear red shirts and white shorts. The Egypt Cup is like the Super Bowl of Egyptian football! It was first played in 1921, the same year that the Egyptian Federation for Football was established, and has been played almost every year since.

Figure it out!

Figure out the answers to these questions about Egyptian football.

1. If a football match is made up of two 45-minute halves with a 15-minute half time, how many minutes will a fan be in the stadium for a match? How many hours?

____

2. The Egyptian Pharaohs won 8 out of 12 games this season. What percent of the games did they lose?

____

Fast Fact:
Egypt's most important football matches are played in the Cairo International Stadium, which is a respected symbol of Egyptian football.

The Nile River— The Heart of Egypt!

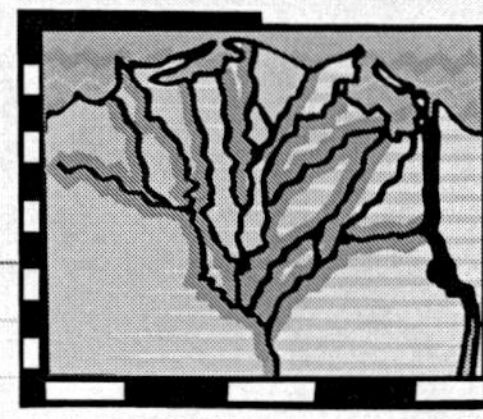

The Nile is the longest river in the world! It stretches 4,000 miles from East Africa to the Mediterranean Sea. The Nile flows from mountains in the south to the Mediterranean in the north. Ancient Egyptians believed that this was the way rivers flowed and considered other rivers to be flowing the wrong way.

The Nile represents life to the people of Egypt, both ancient and modern. For thousands of years, the river has made life possible for people and animals and has shaped the culture.

For many years, the Nile flooded the surrounding valley between June and September due to melting snow and heavy summer rain in the Ethiopian Mountains, which sent the water into the River Nile. Due to the construction of the Aswan Dam in the 1960s, the annual flood was controlled and has not flooded since.

The Nile also supports a vast array of animal life. Most of the animals that live in or around the river are reptiles. The most common reptile is the Nile crocodile. It is the largest crocodile in Africa! The Nile crocodile can be as long as 20 feet and weigh up to 1,500 pounds! The Nile is also home to turtles, lizards, and 15 species of venomous snakes!

The Nile River is important to Egypt and its culture. It is the center of life for both humans and animals alike!

Word Fun!

Place each fact under the column for true or false.

The Nile is the longest river in the world; The Nile has very little animal life; The Nile flows from north to south; The Nile floods every winter; The Nile crocodile can grow up to 20 feet long; The Nile flows into the Mediterranean Sea

True	False

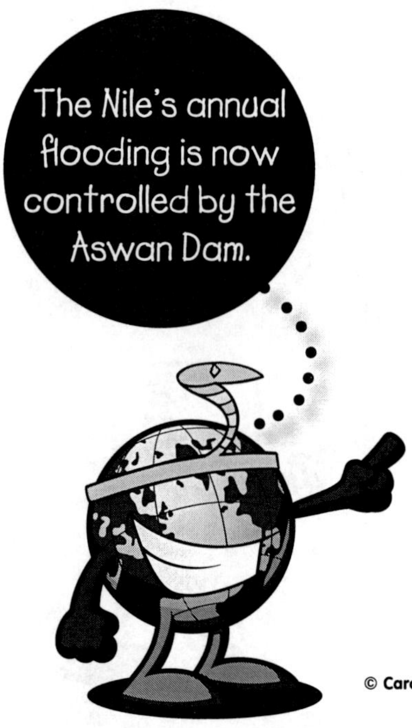

Egypt Did It First!

Word Fun!

This is fun to do with someone else. Ask a friend for words to substitute for the blanks in the story. Their word substitutions will have a humorous effect when the resulting story is then read aloud.

I want to be the first person to ____________ (ACTION VERB)

across ____________ (COUNTRY)! I've been training for this

since ____________ (MONTH). I'm in ____________ (ADJECTIVE) shape.

My ____________ (ADJECTIVE) adventure will begin on

____________ (FAVORITE HOLIDAY). I won't be hard to miss;

I'll be the one wearing a ____________ (COLOR)

____________ (ARTICLE OF CLOTHING) and a pair of matching

____________ (FOOTWEAR). My faithful friends

____________ (FAMOUS ATHLETE) and

____________ (CARTOON CHARACTER) will be there to cheer for me.

I'm bringing my ____________ (NOUN) along for good luck.

I'm confident I'll be the first!

Learning the ABCs Early!
The earliest-known phonetic alphabet was found in Egypt.

Pick a Date, Any Date!
The ancient Egyptians invented the concept of the 365-day calendar.

Take Your Medicine!
The origin of modern medicine was recently discovered to have begun in ancient Egypt.

The Princess Who Became King!
Hatshepsut became Pharaoh of Egypt at a time when Egyptian culture only allowed men to hold that title.

It All Adds Up!
Diophantus, a mathematician, is considered to be the father of algebra.

I Thought My House Was Old!
The Great Pyramid is considered to be the oldest structure in existence and is one of the Seven Wonders of the World.

In late 2011, the leaders of business schools in Africa gathered in Egypt to discuss ways to better their schools' roles in helping the continent deal with food shortages. They also discussed how to deal with African problems more effectively.

One Hump Or Two?

With their long, curved necks and humped backs, camels are perfectly designed to survive in the desert! Camels evolved in North America and crossed the Bering Strait during prehistoric times. Throughout history, camels have been helpers to the people who live in the desert. A camel can carry a load as heavy as 900 pounds!

Some camels have one hump, while others have two. You might have heard that camels store water in their humps. This is not true. The humps are actually made up of fat that provides camels with energy when food is scarce. When a camel's energy is too low, the hump will shrink! The hump returns to normal when the camel restores its energy by eating. Camels store water in their bloodstream! A camel can go five to seven days without a drink of water! The camel's mouth is tough and rubbery, so it can eat thorns and branches. They eat their food whole and allow it to slowly digest.

Word Fun!

Write five questions that would help someone identify a camel if they had never seen one before.

Example: Does this animal have a hump on its back?

1. ____?
2. ____?
3. ____?
4. ____?
5. ____?

Cool Camel Characteristic:

Camels can drink up to 40 gallons of water at once, and their coats reflect sunlight to protect them from the desert heat.

The Valley of the Kings

The Valley of the Kings is filled with dead people! The valley is located on the west bank of the Nile River. For 500 years, tombs were built there for kings and other important Egyptians called "nobles." The valley also holds tombs for the favorite wives and children of both the pharaohs and the nobles.

Construction of a tomb began with each new ruler's reign, and lasted about six years. Tombs were built by cutting through layers of limestone. Most tombs follow the same pattern: three corridors, an antechamber, and a sunken sarcophagus chamber. By the end of the New Kingdom, Egypt had entered a period of political and economic decline. Almost all of the tombs were broken into and robbed. Today the area is a center of archaeological exploration. The tombs still bring researchers from all over the world. The Valley of the Kings is most famous for the discovery of King Tutankhamun's (King Tut) tomb, and is one of the most famous archaeological sites in the world.

Revealing Answer!

Follow the instructions to reveal in which valley most of the tombs are located.

1. Cross off the first and last letters.
2. Cross off any letter "O.
3. Cross off the letter that represents the Roman numeral 10.
4. Cross off the seventh letter of the alphabet.
5. Cross off the third letter from the right.
6. Cross off the last letter of the alphabet.

YEAXSOT VXAGLOLZEQYR

The Suez Canal

Suez Canal

KABOOM!! The fireworks that exploded in the air above Egypt in November of 1869 celebrated the opening of the Suez Canal. The canal was a manmade waterway that connected the Mediterranean Sea and the Red Sea. This passageway allowed ships traveling between Europe and Africa to take a shortcut through Egypt instead of sailing all the way around Africa. This meant that companies could save time and money shipping their products around the world.

It took 10 years and $100 million to build the canal! More than 6,000 guests attended the opening celebration! Egypt shared ownership of the canal with France, but Egypt soon fell into financial trouble and sold its rights to Great Britain. This gave Great Britain enormous power and influence over Egypt. Eventually, Great Britain invaded and conquered Egypt. In 1967, after Egypt gained its independence, it fought in the Six-Day war and decided to shut down the canal. The war only lasted four days in Egypt, but the canal stayed closed until 1975. It is still open today, making way for ships from all over the world!

Cross it off!
Starting with the first letter, cross off every other letter to reveal the name of the piece of land the Suez Canal runs through.

AICSHTUHIMLUPSJOFFTSYUHEJZ

____

As unrest grew in Egypt and the Arab countries in early 2011, some feared that any blockage of the Suez Canal could create chaos in world shipping.

Howard Carter and the Curse of King Tut

Egyptian King Tutankhamun began ruling when he was 8 or 9 years old and mysteriously died at the young age of 19. It is thought that his enemies murdered him. After his death, his name was removed from all the record books as if he never existed! It seemed as though he would never make it into the history books.

In 1891, a young Englishman named Howard Carter journeyed to Egypt to search for the tomb of a king whose name he had seen on some stone walls. Carter dug for five years. Finally, on November 4, 1922, Carter's workmen uncovered a step. Then they discovered 15 more! These steps led to an ancient doorway! Inside the tomb was a gold coffin with the mummy of King Tutankhamun! It was a day of joy and celebration! No one seemed to remember the warning Carter had been given about a curse on the tomb.

A few months after the tomb was opened, the man who had funded Carter's research suddenly died. By 1929, 11 people connected with the discovery of the tomb had died. Today, most experts believe that the deaths were probably caused by a fungus inside the tomb. Are the experts of today correct, or is there really a curse on anyone who disturbs the king's tomb? We will never know!

Did you know?
It is said that on the outside of King Tut's tomb are engraved the words: "Death shall come on swift wings to him who disturbs the peace of the king..."!

Figure it out!
Make a list of the things you might find in a tomb and a list of things you might take on an archaeological dig.

Dig	**Tomb**
Example: a shovel	**Example: a mummy**
______________	______________
______________	______________
______________	______________
______________	______________

In the 2011 demonstrations, Egyptians joined arms to surround the main museum in Cairo and protect the priceless King Tut treasures. Unfortunately, some artifacts were destroyed by looters, but it is believed that others may be able to be repaired.

Sarcophagus - The Last Thing You'll Ever Wear!

It might sound like the name for a bad cold, but a sarcophagus is really a stone container built to hold a coffin of ancient Egyptian royalty! In the Egyptian language, the word "sarcophagus" translates to "possessor of life." The ancient Egyptians believed in an afterlife, and the sarcophagus was seen as the outer layer of protection for the royalty inside. An ancient Egyptian sarcophagus was decorated on the outside with detailed paintings and carvings. A typical sarcophagus was engraved with hieroglyphs on both the inside and the outside. Early forms of sarcophagi (more than one sarcophagus!) were designed to represent the palaces of the pharaoh. Later versions were made to resemble the shape of the pharaoh inside, complete with a carved portrait of the head!

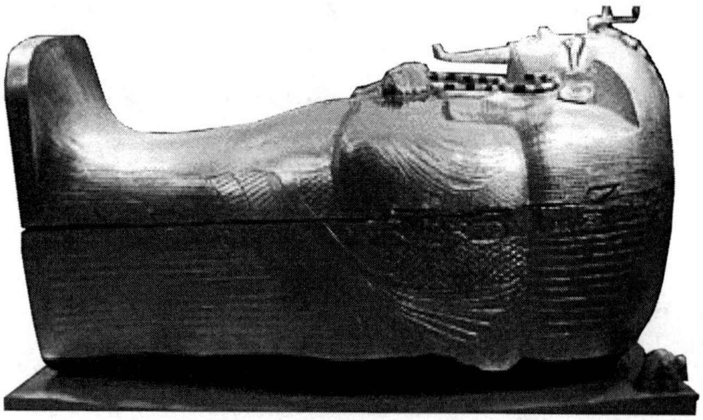

Materials used to make the sarcophagi ranged from stone to solid gold. They were equipped with sleds, so oxen could drag them across the desert to the site of the tomb!

Know your facts!

Next to each statement below, write F for Fact, and FIC for Fiction.

_____ 1. A sarcophagus is a container for a coffin.

_____ 2. The word "sarcophagus" translates to "coffin" in the Egyptian language.

_____ 3. Early sarcophagi were made of iron ore.

_____ 4. Egyptian sarcophagi were decorated with paintings and carvings.

_____ 5. Later versions of sarcophagi were carved in the form of a family member's head.

_____ 6. Sarcophagi were moved by sleds.

Assorted Architecture!

Figure it out!

Use the following clues to figure out the name of this famous building in Alexandria, Egypt!

- This structure was one of the Seven Wonders of the Ancient World.
- The structure's designer put a secret inscription of his own name on the structure even after the pharaoh told him not to!
- Finished in 260 B.C.E., it was built to be a symbol to the world and as a guide to bring ships into the busy harbor.
- It was built on the island of Pharos and soon took the name Pharos for itself.
- Originally, it stood somewhere between 450 and 600 feet high, one of the tallest buildings of its time except for the Great Pyramid.
- It became an ancient world tourist attraction. If tourists wanted, they could climb to the top tower and see the view from 300 feet above the sea!

Talk Like an Egyptian!

Here are a few Egyptian words you may already know.

amulet: good luck charm

arabic: language spoken in Egypt

bazaar: outdoor shopping area

bedouin: nomadic desert people

begah: a woman's headscarf

dynasty: a period of time a certain group of rulers were in power

galabiyya: long smock

hieroglyph: symbol that means a letter, sound or word

kohl: thick black paint; often used as eye makeup

mosque: Muslim place of worship

mummification: process of preserving a dead body

mummy: human or animal that has been embalmed, preserved, and wrapped in cloth

oasis: area of water, plants, and trees in the midst of a desert

obelisk: four-sided tapered tower with a pyramid-shaped top

papyrus: paper made from the stem of a plant

____

____

____

____

Further Resources

US Embassy in Cairo
8 Kamal El Din Salah St.
Garden City, Cairo, Egypt
Phone: 20-2-2797-3300

United Nations
2 United Nations Plaza
New York, NY 10017

Egyptian Tourist Authority
Misr Travel Tower, Abbassia Square
Cairo, Egypt
Phone: 285-4509/284-1970
Fax: 285-4363
http://www.egypt.travel

Interesting Websites

www.ancientegypt.co.uk

www.alexandriaegypt.com/

http://www.kingtut.org

http://familyinternet.about.com/od/websites/a/pyramids-of-egypt.htm

Answer Key

Page 7
1. flag 2. official 3. Africa's 4. pound
5. calendar 6. Cairo

Page 8
1. c. 2. a.

Page 9

Page 10
3, 6, 2, 4, 7, 1, 5

Page 11
1. C 2. F 3. E 4. A 5. B 6. D

Page 12
Cats-E, Cholera Epidemics-D, Scarabs-B,
Mummification-A, 10 Plagues of Egypt-C

Page 17

akhdar	green
ab	father
harr	hot
gadaa	lunch
Adar	March
matihaf	museum
la	no
Nofember	November
ahmar	red
salata	salad

Page 21
1. 105 minutes, 1.75 hours (1 hour and 45 minutes)
2. 33% (1/3 of the games)

Page 22
True
The Nile is the longest river in the world.
The Nile crocodile can grow up to 20 feet long.
The Nile flows into the Mediterranean Sea.

False
The Nile has very little animal life.
The Nile flows from north to south.
The Nile floods every winter.

Page 25
East Valley

Page 26
Isthmus of Suez

Page 28
1. F, 2. FIC, 3. FIC, 4. F, 5. F, 6. F

Page 29
Lighthouse at Alexandria